AF428209

Follow Us On Social Media

Get Connected With Our Latest News And Updates

 on Instagram @coreconnection.llc

on Facebook @Core Connection

on Google @coreconnection-llc.com

on Email info@coreconnection-llc.com

HOW TO DEVELOP A GROWTH MINDSET

01 — Identify Your Mindset

02 — Set Clear Goals

03 — Seek Feedback NOT Approval

04 — Harness The Power Of 'YET'

05 — Challenges As Opportunities

06 — Book Review

Concept 1

Growth vs Fixed Mindset

WHAT IS A
FIXED MINDSET

A fixed mindset is a mindset where people believe their traits are set and have a limit.

A fixed mindset is a mindset where people believe they can not learn from their challenges and setbacks.

A fixed mindset is a mindset where people stick to what they know and don't explore and expand their knowledge.

W H A T   I S   A
GROWTH MINDSET

A growth mindset is a mindset where people believe they can always expand and grow.

A growth mindset is a mindset where people believe that through hard work and dedication our abilities can build and strengthen.

A growth mindset is a mindset where people believe their behaviors and attitudes are not fixed.

20
Growth Mindset Questions
to ask yourself

1. What made me think hard today?
2. How will I challenge myself today?
3. How can I overcome my fears so I can reach my goals?
4. What can I learn from this mistake?
5. What do I want to learn?
6. What strategies can I try?
7. How can I turn a struggle into a learning experience?
8. How is a fixed mindset holding me back?
9. Do I hold myself to a high standard?
10. What is the next challenge to tackle?
11. Do I ask for help when I need it?
12. Am I kind and willing to help others?
13. What is the best way I can build trust with someone?
14. How do my actions show whether I am a good or bad listener?
15. What about my mindset would I like to change?
16. How does self-reflecting help me grow?
17. How does my attitude affect my performance?
18. What does success mean to me?
19. Who can I lean on when I need support?
20. What did I learn from a recent setback/disappointment?

GROWTH OR FIXED MINDSET WORKSHEET

Instructions: Identify which phrases indicate a fixed or growth mindset.

		GROWTH MINDSET	FIXED MINDSET
1.	I'm not good at this		
2.	I love challenges		
3.	I don't like it when I make mistakes		
4.	This is too difficult		
5.	Practice makes perfect		
6.	I want to try again		
7.	When I get frustrated, I persevere		
8.	I can always improve, so I'll keep trying		
9.	When I fail, I learn		
10.	I'll never be as smart as her		

Instructions: Re-write each of the phrases below in the correct column.

Fixed Mindset	Growth Mindset
Example: I can't improve.	Example: I can improve.

I can't do this.

I need help understanding this.

It will take some time to get this.

I can learn from this mistake.

I'm not good at this.

I'll never get any better at this.

This is too hard.

I'll try it a different way.

I don't have it 'yet'.

<u>FLIP</u> YOUR FIXED MINDSET AND <u>FLOP</u> TO A GROWTH MINDSET

INSTRUCTIONS: DRAW A LINE TO A FLIP FLOP FOR EACH PHRASE THAT DEMONSTRATES HOW TO FLIP YOUR FIXED MINDSET. EACH FLIP FLOP SHOULD ONLY HAVE ONE LINE DRAWN TO IT.

It is too hard to change

I can't change my perspectives

believe your way is the only way

hard work and dedication

expand your thinking

narrow your thinking

explore new avenues for knowledge

persevere through challenges

don't discover new opportunities

learn from setbacks

stop if a challenge gets in your way

Reset your mindset

Define In Your Own Words

Growth Mindset

Fixed Mindset

Identifying Your Mindset

Use the chart below to reflect on your mindset.

COMPREHEND

What about your behavior and personality do you know for sure?

CHANGE

What about your behavior do you want to make improvements?

COMBAT

What strategies can you use to make improvements?

GROWTH VS FIXED MINDSET
DISSCUSSION QUESTIONS

Instructions: Answer the questions below

What is a fixed mindset?

What is a growth mindset?

Why is having a growth mindset important?

How can having a growth mindset help you succeed?

What is a growth mindset question you can ask yourself?

If you find yourself having a fixed mindset what can you tell yourself to flip it?

YOU GOT THIS
Trust The
Process!

Concept 2

Setting Clear Goals

HOW DO WE SET GOALS?

S.M.A.R.T goal setting is a way to set clear, achievable goals! Below is what S.M.A.R.T stands for.

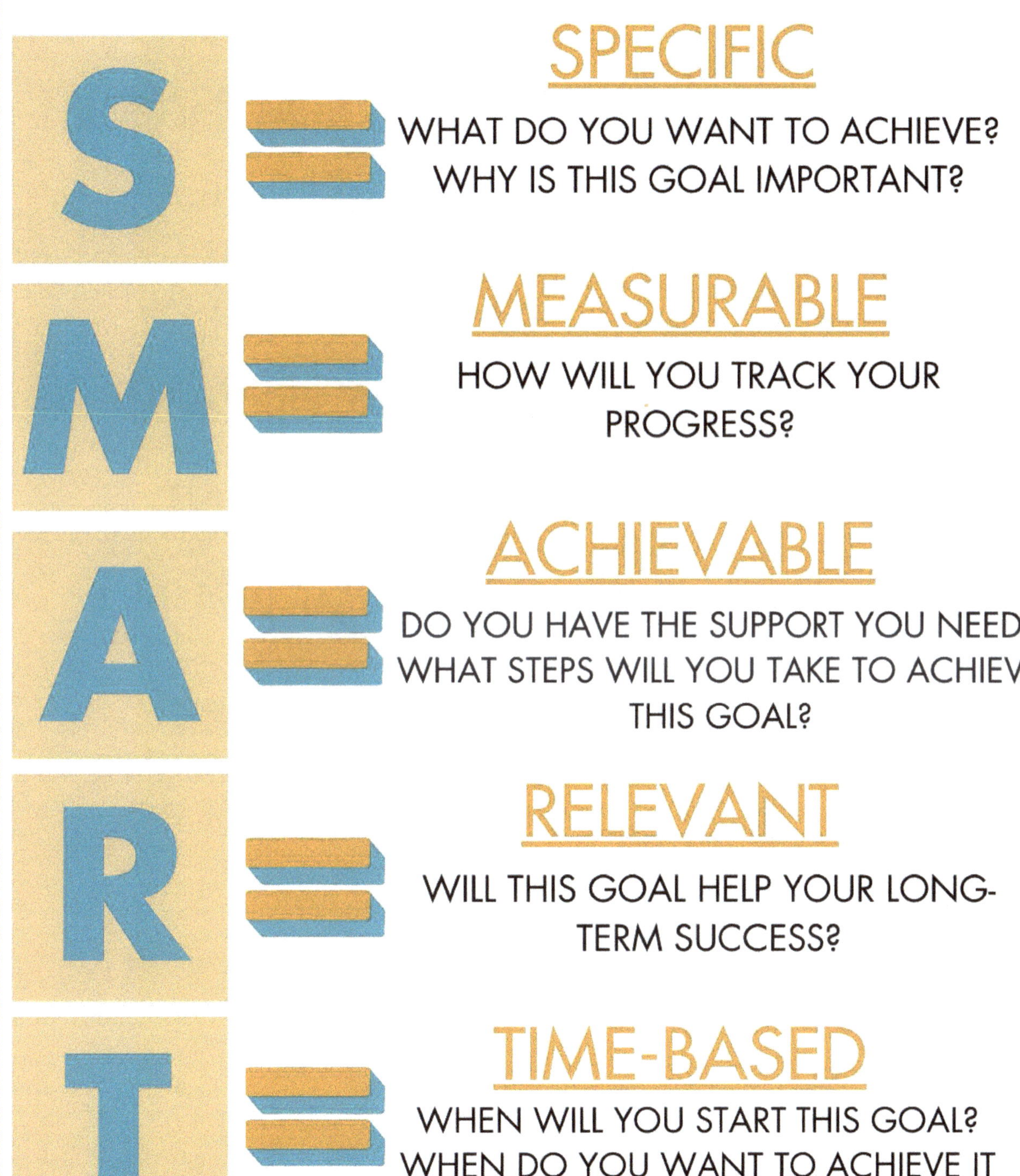

GOAL SETTING PRACTICE

WHAT IS YOUR GOAL?

WHY IS THIS GOAL IMPORTANT?

WHEN DO YOU WANT TO ACHIEVE THIS GOAL?

WHAT IS NEEDED TO ACHIEVE THIS GOAL?

SMART GOAL CHECKLIST

- ○ SPECIFIC
- ○ MEASURABLE
- ○ ACHIEVABLE
- ○ RELEVANT
- ○ TIME-BOUND

WHAT ARE POTENTIAL CHALLENGES?

A letter to my future self!

Instructions: Writing a letter to your future self is a fun activity to practice using SMART goals. When writing your letter to yourself include things like advice to yourself, your wildest dreams, predictions about what your life will look like in the future, and highlights of your life today.

Dear,_______

____

____

____

____

____

____

____

____

____

____

Love,

Long Term Goal Setting

Long term goals are achieved by completing a combination of short term goals.

Instructions: In the center of the flower write your long-term goal. In the petals write short term goals that will help you achieve it. When you complete each step color your flower in accordingly. Once your flower is completely colored you have accomplished your long-term goal.

Short Term Goal Setting

Short term goals are made up of even smaller goals.

Instructions: In the center of each flower, write the short-term goals from the previous page. On each petal, write steps for achieving this goal. Color in the steps as you complete your goals.

GOAL STRATEGIES

Ways I can work towards my goals	Ways I can work past obstacles	Ways to prioritize my health while achieving my goals	Ways to keep me motivated while achieving my goals
☆	☆	☆	☆
☆	☆	☆	☆
☆	☆	☆	☆
☆	☆	☆	☆

GOAL SETTING IS IMPORTANT BECAUSE...

it focuses your energy toward what you want and what is most important to you. This increases your CONFIDENCE in the belief that you can succeed. Instructions: color the page while thinking about just how amazing you are!

S.M.A.R.T GOAL

Instructions: Fill in the dotted line with what each letter stands for.

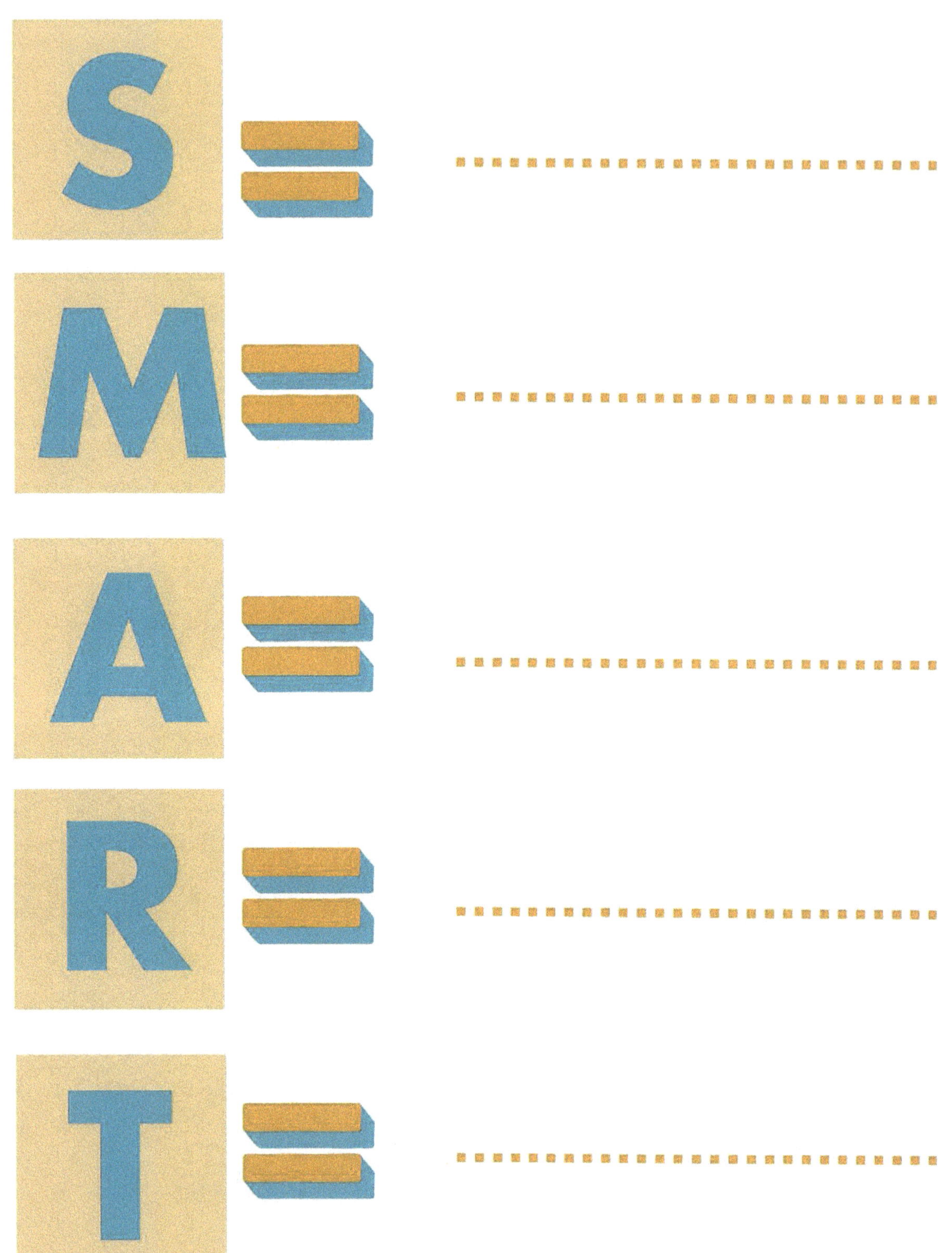

GOAL SETTING DISCUSSION QUESTIONS

INSTRUCTIONS: ANSWER THE QUESTIONS ABOUT SMART GOALS BELOW.

HOW DOES GOAL SETTING HELP YOU SUCCEED?

HOW DOES GOAL SETTING AND HAVING A GROWTH MINDSET RELATE?

HOW DOES HAVING GOAL STRATEGIES IMPROVE YOUR OVERALL WELLBEING?

WHY DOES USING SMART GOALS HELP US CREATE QUALITY GOALS?

YOU ARE DOING GREAT
Keep Going!

Concept 3
Seeking Feedback

SEEKING FEEDBACK

allows you to determine if you are improving and whether your behaviors align with your goals.

Seeking feedback is part of building your growth mindset because it helps identify where you can improve both physically and mentally.

NOT APPROVAL

Feedback means seeking information to improve yourself not to get validation for your efforts or successes.

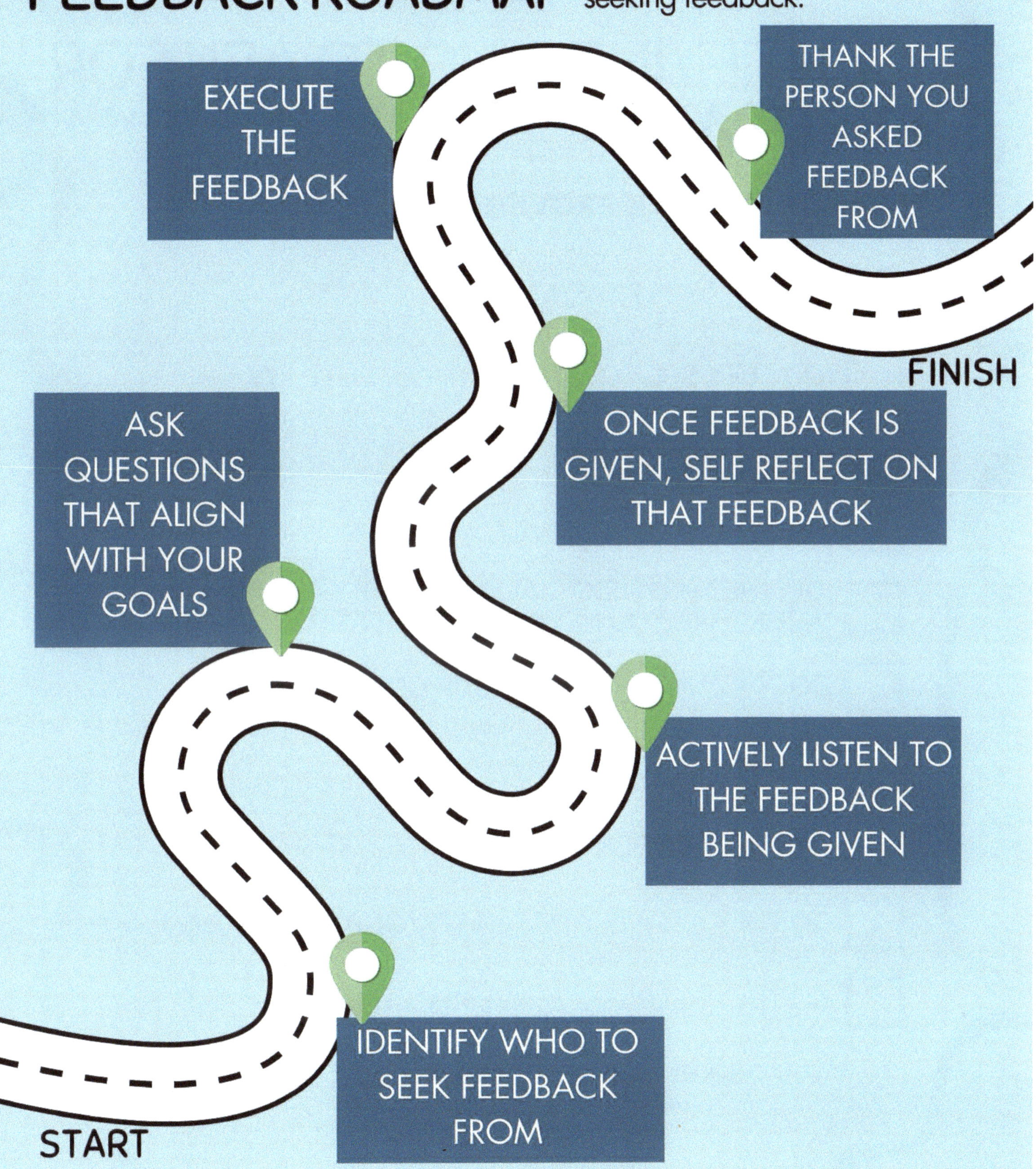
HOW TO SEEK FEEDBACK ROADMAP
Instructions: Trace the dotted line to learn the steps of seeking feedback.
EXECUTE THE FEEDBACK
THANK THE PERSON YOU ASKED FEEDBACK FROM
ASK QUESTIONS THAT ALIGN WITH YOUR GOALS
ONCE FEEDBACK IS GIVEN, SELF REFLECT ON THAT FEEDBACK
FINISH
ACTIVELY LISTEN TO THE FEEDBACK BEING GIVEN
IDENTIFY WHO TO SEEK FEEDBACK FROM
START

IDENTIFYING WHO TO ASK FOR FEEDBACK

INSTRUCTIONS: CHECK THE BOXES THAT DESCRIBE WHO YOUR FEEDBACK PROVIDER IS.

NAME OF FEEDBACK PROVIDER: ______________________

- ☐ DO YOU TRUST THEM?
- ☐ DO THEY SPEAK TO YOU WITH POSITIVITY?
- ☐ ARE THEY HONEST?
- ☐ ARE THEY SUPPORTIVE?
- ☐ DO THEY HAVE EXPERIENCE IN THE SPECIFIC AREA THAT YOU NEED FEEDBACK FOR?
- ☐ DO THEY UNDERSTAND YOUR GOALS?
- ☐ DO THEY RESPECT YOU?
- ☐ ARE THEY PATIENT?
- ☐ DO THEY ACTIVELY LISTEN TO YOUR QUESTIONS?
- ☐ DO THEY HELP YOU SOLVE PROBLEMS?

*IF YOU CHECKED 7 OUT OF 10 BOXES THIS PERSON IS A GOOD PERSON TO ASK FOR FEEDBACK

Mirror, Mirror on the wall, who's the fairest feedback provider of them all ?

Instructions: Use the mirror below to write all of the people you would ask for feedback from.

ACTIVE LISTENING LADDER

TIPS AND TRICKS

6 Do not interrupt the speaker, take your turn

5 Face the speaker and make eye contact

4 Stay focused on their words

3 Do not start planning on what to say next

2 Respond without judgement or opinions

1 Give the speaker your undivided attention

READ THE PROMPT

and self-reflect if you were Jane to answer the questions on the next page

---

You had a really challenging practice. You felt tired and your body was aching a bit. Your coach noticed you having a few falls in a row and asked how you were doing. At first, you said you were fine and ready for the rest of practice.

When you moved to the floor, you were still struggling and not doing as well as usual. Your coach called you over and asked you to be honest about how you were feeling. This time, you told the truth—you felt heavy, tired, and your body just wasn't up for it that day.

Your coach put their hand on your shoulder and shared some advice. They said it's important to be honest because then we can work together to come up with a different practice plan. They explained that on days when you're not at your best, it's okay to give 80%, and we can adjust things to make sure you feel better and rested for the next practice.

You thanked your coach for the feedback and finished the rest of practice with an adjusted plan. While it was hard to tell your coach you were not at your best today you self-reflected and realized the importance of honesty and communication.

Guided Self-Reflection Practice

Self-reflection is having quiet time to yourself where you think deeply about who you are, your actions, and your emotions.

Instructions: Follow the prompt you read on the previous page and answer the questions to practice self-reflection on feedback.

Asking yourself questions like these allows you to self-reflect any scenario that might occur!

EXECUTING THE FEEDBACK

INSTRUCTIONS: Let's brainstorm ways to execute feedback you were given by your coach.

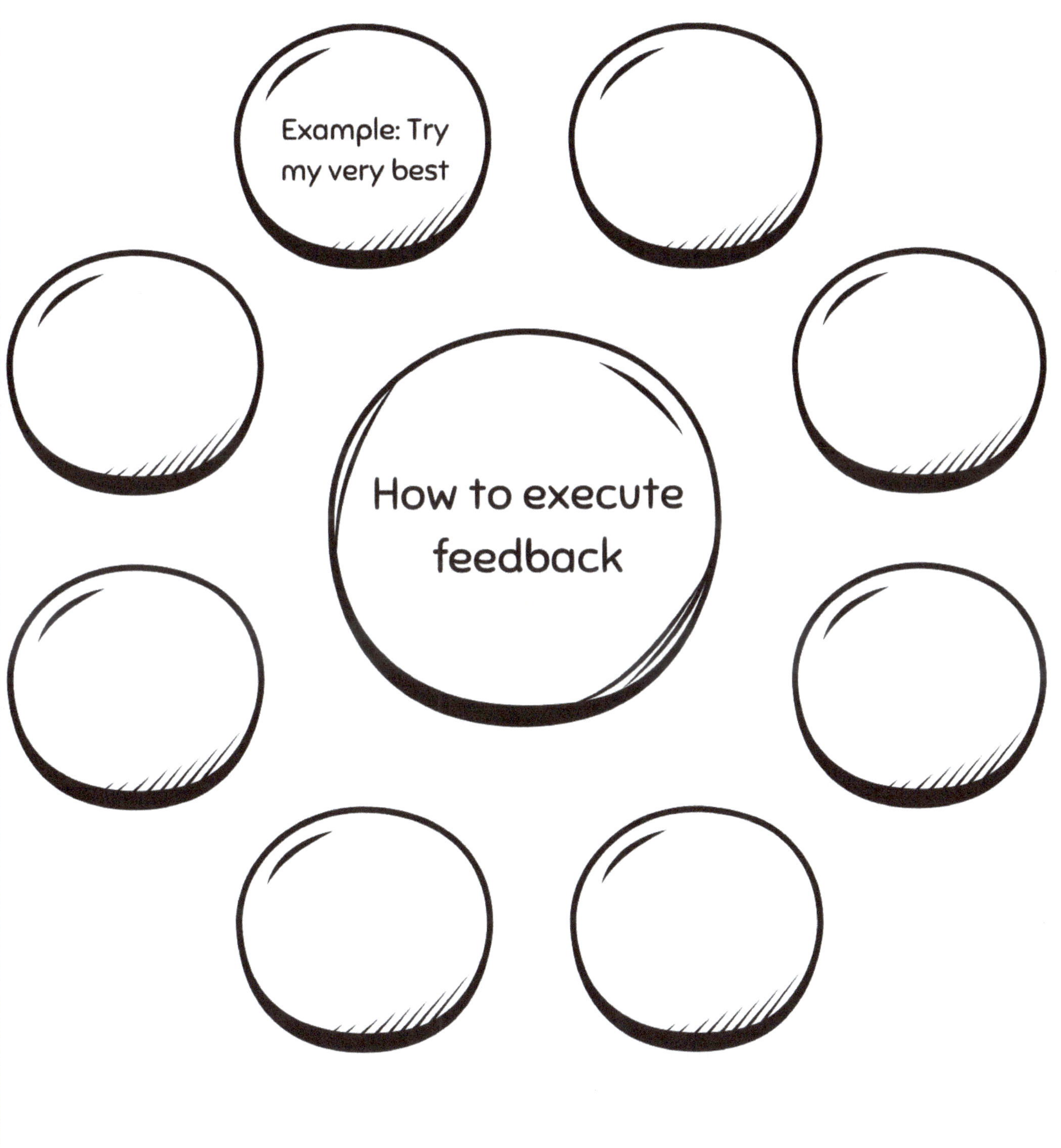

SEEKING FEEDBACK DISCUSSION QUESTIONS

INSTRUCTIONS: ANSWER THE QUESTIONS BELOW

1. How is finding someone with good character traits important in seeking feedback?

2. Why is executing the feedback important?

3. Why is active listening important?

4. How is self-reflecting on feedback important to your growth?

KEEP UP THE GOOD WORK
KEEP UP THE GOOD WORK
You Rock!

Concept 4

The Power of Yet

The POWER of...

YET

SUPERHERO CAPABILITIES

RESETS YOUR MINDSET
IMPROVES POSITIVE THINKING
EXPRESSES THE VALUE OF PERSEVERANCE

Harnessing the **POWER** of **YET**

Instructions: read the sentences and fill in the blank with 'yet'. See how the sentence changes into opportunity.

1. I can't do this

2. I'm not good at this

3. I do not understand this

4. This doesn't make sense

5. I can't do it without help

6. I haven't learned how to

Instructions: Answer the question below.
How will you use the word 'yet' to strengthen your growth mindset?

____

____

____

____

__________'s Power of yet

Draw a picture of something you are learning and then fill in the blanks.

I can't

____

____

YET

BUT...

I can _______________

I can _______________

I can _______________

READ THE PROMPT

In the small gym of Possibility, a wise coach gathered their eager athletes to share a secret that would change their lives. "Listen closely," the coach began, "for I shall teach you the power of yet."

With curious eyes, the coach explained, "Whenever you face a challenge or find yourself saying, 'I can't do this,' simply add the word 'yet' at the end. Suddenly, the door to endless possibilities swings wide open." The athletes exchanged glances, intrigued. The coach continued, "You see, 'yet' transforms impossibilities into realities and limitations into opportunities. 'I can't do this' becomes 'I can't do this yet,' and in that tiny word lies the power of growth and endless potential."

And so, armed with the power of "yet," the athletes embarked on their journeys, turning setbacks into stepping stones and challenges into opportunities for learning and discovery. In the gym of Possibility, the athletes learned how much hope the power of the word "yet" holds. It became a reminder that every challenge was merely the start to what could be.

ANSWER THE QUESTIONS

and ponder how the power of yet could change your life

How do you think being armed with the power of yet helps the athletes succeed?

How does the word yet transform limitations into opportunities?

Why do you think the coach told the athletes this secret?

When should the athletes use the word yet to reset their mindset?

Going from "I can't" to "I can't yet"

1 What I think I can't do

2 Why I think that

3 Why I should try

4 What is holding me back

Power of Yet Word Search

A	D	C	H	A	L	L	E	N	G	E
E	S	B	H	F	P	O	I	T	I	V
V	P	U	O	N	C	G	T	A	O	B
I	L	H	P	O	F	Y	E	C	P	G
T	F	Y	E	E	G	A	S	L	V	R
I	N	O	A	V	R	H	E	C	Y	O
S	V	C	H	S	B	P	R	W	F	W
O	D	G	W	A	Y	C	O	A	F	T
P	B	L	L	F	W	F	Y	W	T	H
N	H	C	V	M	I	N	D	S	E	T
E	F	F	E	C	T	I	V	E	Y	R

growth　　　　mindset　　　　effective

hope　　　　challenge　　　　reset

superpower　　　　yet　　　　positive

THE POWER OF YET
DISCUSSION QUESTIONS

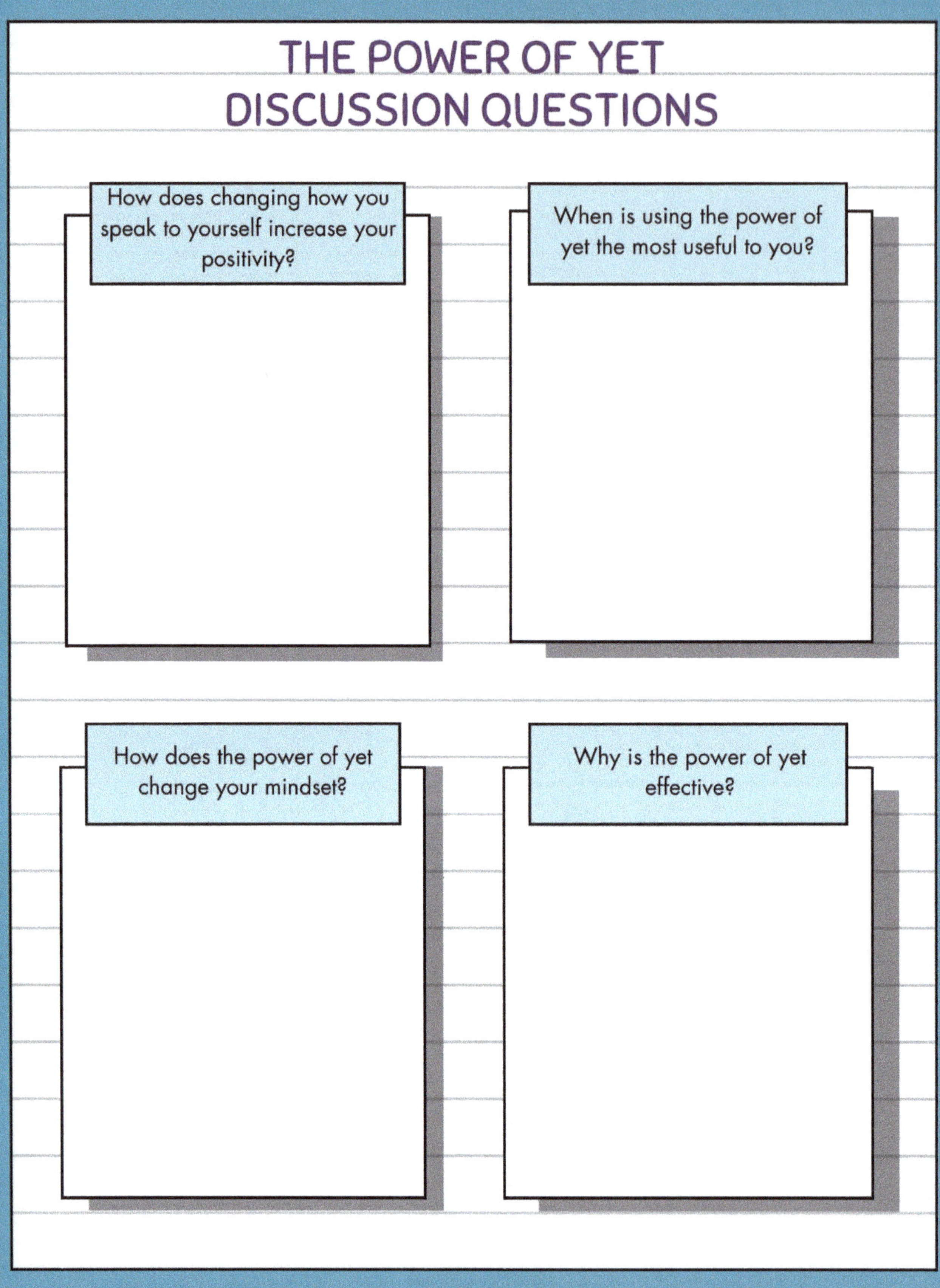

Don't
Give Up!
TAKE CARE OF YOUR MIND

Concept 5

Challenges As Opportunities

8 TIPS FOR OVERCOMING FEARS AND OBSTACLES

YOUR SUPER STRENGTHS

Instructions: Circle the top 5 characteristics that you have.

PERSEVERANCE	OPEN MINDED
GRATITUDE	BRAVE
KINDESS	CONFIDENT
COMMUNICATIVE	CURIOUS
LOVING	HONEST
INTELLIGENT	INDEPENDENT
CREATIVE	RESILIENT
FAIRNESS	HUMOROUS
TEAMWORK	LEADERSHIP
FORGIVENESS	CALM
HOPE	CHEERFUL
COOPERATIVE	THOUGHTFUL
HARD-WORKING	ADVENTUROUS

Instructions: Write how you demonstrate the characteristics you circled.

IDENTIFYING STRENGTHS
SHIELD

Instructions: fill in the shield and then reflect on your strengths

Knowing your strengths will help you utilize them to overcome challenges

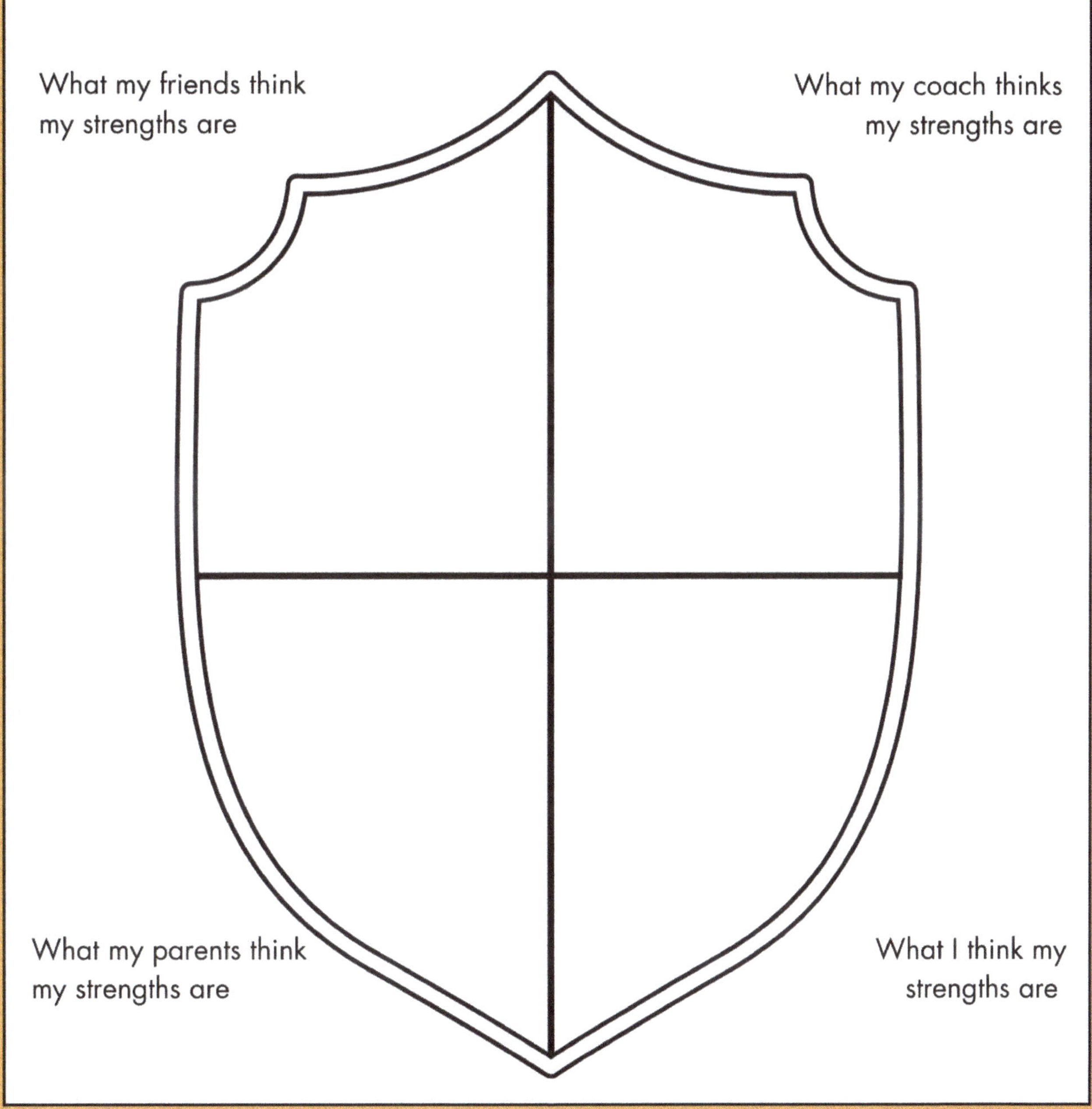

CHALLENGES
AND EMOTIONS

Instructions: Write your challenge in the designated bubble and the way it makes you feel in the emotion bubbles, then answer the questions below.

CHALLENGE

EMOTION

EMOTION

EMOTION

How do your emotions impact you in your challenges?

How do positive emotions towards challenges help you overcome them?

I CHALLENGE YOU...

Instructions: Finish the sentences below.

I do my best when I feel...

When I struggle I feel...

When I am frustrated I...

If I am overwhelmed I...

I am comfortable when...

When I am out of my comfort zone I feel...

I calm my nerves by...

I overcome struggles by...

Self-reflecting on these answers when you are struggling can help you identify what is holding you back and allow changes in your mindset to overcome the challenges you are facing.

Accepting Challenges

Instructions: Find a way through the maze and then answer the question at the end.

Notice hitting a dead end did not stop you from getting to the other side. Accepting that you were going to hit a challenge allowed you to get to the end with positive emotions. Imagine if this was YOUR challenge and you hit a dead end, how does looking at this dead end with gratitude allow you to try again?

____

____

____

How to look at obstacles as opportunities

Instructions: Write down your obstacles and for each obstacle write what opportunity it brings.

Obstacles	Opportunities

Attitude of Gratitude

Instructions: In the jar write down everything you are grateul for and then answer the question below!

How does the attitude of gratitude change your thoughts on challenges?

Challenges as Opportunities
Discussion Questions

How can negative emotions towards challenges show you areas where your mindset needs improvement?

How does identifying your strengths help you get through a challenge?

How can you use your knowledge of your strengths and weaknesses to help get you through challenges and obstacles?

How can you use gratitude as a tool to change your negative emotions about challenges into more positive ones?

Overall, how does accepting challenges as opportunities allow you to reach your goals?

YOU ARE ALMOST DONE
Stay
Focused!

Book Review

GROWTH MINDSET BOOK REVIEW

What strategies can you use to develop a growth mindset?

How does a growth mindset help you in your day to day life?

How does setting clear goals help you achieve them?

How does goal setting increase your confidence?

GROWTH MINDSET BOOK REVIEW

How does knowing your strengths and weaknesses help you overcome challenges?

Why is the attitude of gratitude so important?

List the concepts in order from which one you liked the most to the one you liked the least?

What activity or worksheet was the most fun and why?

GROWTH MINDSET BOOK REVIEW

How does a growth mindset help you achieve your goals?

Why is it important to actively listen?

What are the six active listening tips and tricks?

Why is feedback important?

GROWTH MINDSET BOOK REVIEW

How does the power of yet reset your mindset?

What are the power of yet's superhero capabilities?

How are challenges learning opportunities?

What are the best ways to handle obstacles?

Proud
of
You!